BUYING AUTO INSURANCE IN MICHIGAN

EVERYTHING YOU NEED TO KNOW ABOUT MICHIGAN'S NEW NO FAULT LAWS

The Best Choices To Help Protect You And Your Family From The Fallout Of An Auto Accident

JOSEPH T. BARBERI

Michigan Auto Accident Attorney

BARBERI LAW

EVERY CASE WE TAKE,
WE TAKE PERSONALLY.®

2305 HAWTHORN DRIVE, STE C,
MT. PLEASANT, MI 48858

989-773-3423
1-800-336-3423
WWW.BARBERILAWFIRM.COM

ISBN: 978-1-63385-372-0

Designed and published by
Word Association Publishers

205 Fifth Avenue
Tarentum, Pennsylvania 15084
www.wordassociation.com
1.800.827.7903

FOREWORD
—Rowan Barberi, Age 6

Joe Barberi is my Papa. He always tries to help people when they get hurt. His book is about protecting people when they get into a bad accident. Since I'm only in Kindergarten and just learning to read, some of Papa's book will be better understood by you. I think you will be happy you read Papa's book. And if you have any questions, I know Papa will answer them — he's always there for me when I need him, and I'm sure he'll be there for you too — if you need him

Sincerely,

Rowan Barberi

In Michigan, after 46 years of No-Fault Auto Insurance, consumers are now faced with making all kinds of new difficult choices when it comes to selecting options to protect themselves and their household family members under Michigan's new No-Fault Laws adopted June 11, 2019, and scheduled to become effective July 1, 2020!

LEGAL DISCLAIMER

This book is designed to educate consumers contemplating purchasing auto insurance in Michigan. This book is ***not*** intended to give legal advice. This book was written for educational purposes only.

To obtain legal advice, which is specific to you or your business, I strongly recommend that you meet and consult with either a knowledgeable local insurance agent or with an attorney who is up to date on Michigan's new No Fault laws. If you wish to consult with Mr. Barberi or a member of his legal team regarding a specific motor vehicle accident or to review your auto insurance policy, his contact information is found at the end of this book or you can reach out to his legal team at barberilawfirm.com.

CONTENTS

INTRODUCTION

New insurance laws are scheduled to take effect July 1, 2020, which will govern the treatment of individuals who have purchased Michigan auto insurance and then become involved in motor vehicle accidents. Both the injured, and those who cause another's injuries, will be affected by the decisions Michigan consumers make when selecting coverage options available under Michigan's new No-Fault insurance policies.

WARNING

Only **you** can protect yourself and your family from the fallout of being involved in a serious motor vehicle accident where you or others are critically injured. Neither the State of Michigan nor another responsible driver can be counted on to offer you and your family members adequate protection from being the victim of a life altering injury (or from being sued for causing a catastrophic injury to another individual).

This book provides the reader with information with the goal of fostering the best possible decisions when it comes to understanding the "whys" behind choices that will be offered to consumers when purchasing auto insurance under Michigan's new No-Fault laws.

In such regard, this book will focus on 4 subject areas:

1. Understanding insurance terms and the different kinds of losses that can be covered by Michigan insurance policies.
2. Understanding why purchasing adequate motor vehicle insurance coverage in Michigan is more important than ever before.

3. Understanding the various types of new insurance coverage options available under Michigan's new No-Fault laws.

4. Understanding how you can best purchase adequate auto insurance coverage at a competitive price.

As a Michigan attorney who has over 30 years of experience handling motor vehicle accident cases, I can assure you that being adequately insured is probably **the most important** thing you can do to protect yourself and your family in the event of being involved in motor vehicle accident.

Here are some of the reasons why:

a. People are genuinely shocked when they are left to face the effects of permanent injuries that restrict their ability to lead their normal lives in the future. Sadly, such injuries occur to individuals who may have been totally innocent in causing the accident, and the at-fault driver has complied with Michigan's mandatory minimum insurance coverage responsibilities ($50,000/$100,000).

b. People become upset when they are told that they have to pay for another driver's mistake and that their payments will have to be made out of their own pockets (even if they don't have the ability to do so). Injured individuals can be forced into bankruptcy or to go on Welfare through no fault of their own.

c. It's heartbreaking to see how, in a split second, a person's life can be devastated due to somebody else being at fault even though the injured person thought that they had purchased adequate insurance coverage that protected themselves from someone else's negligence.

d. Michigan has dramatically changed its approach to handling reimbursement for medical-related ex-penses for individuals seriously injured in a motor vehicle accident.

e. A large percentage of individuals will now have reimbursement for their medical-related expenses capped at low amounts, such that if they are seriously injured, their insurance coverage for medical-related expenses will be exhausted, many before they even leave the hospital after an accident.

f.   Additionally, now more than ever before, you also need to protect yourself in the event that you seriously injure another individual in a motor vehicle accident that was caused by your fault.

BEWARE

Even if you are completely innocent causing a motor vehicle accident, you can get stuck with thousands, or even hundreds of thousands of dollars of medical bills, and experience a permanent future loss of income while receiving permanent restrictions on your ability to lead your normal life. All of these effects of a motor vehicle accident can be devastating. And those loved ones who depended on you for your financial support can be left out in the cold with no recourse but to go on public assistance. One of the main purposes of this book is to help you make the best decisions to protect you and your family members from having these devastating outcomes.

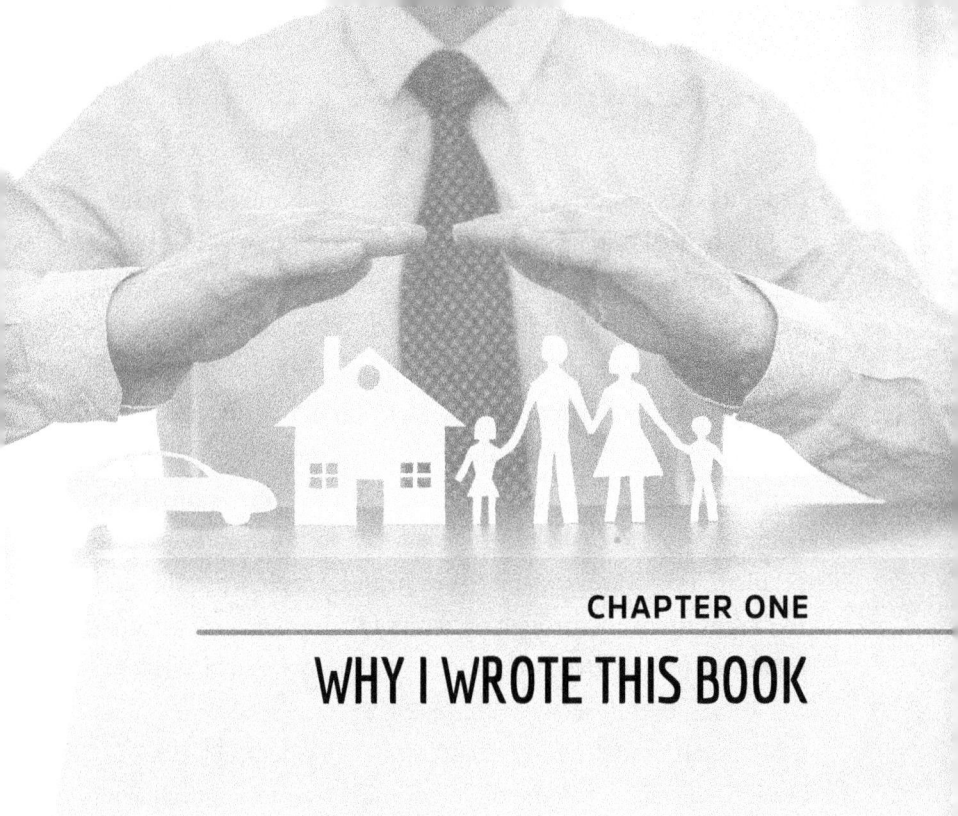

CHAPTER ONE

WHY I WROTE THIS BOOK

I was inspired to write this book after reading a book written by Florida accident attorney, Jeffrey L. Meldon, Esq., the owner and principal attorney of Meldon Law. Mr. Meldon is a well-respected auto accident attorney practicing personal injury law in Florida. If any of the readers themselves suffer an auto accident in the State of Florida or know of a loved one who incurs injuries from a motor vehicle accident in Florida, I recommend Meldon Law, whose main office is located in Gainesville, Florida, to assist you or them in seeking compensation for you or their injuries. Additionally, I thank Mr. Meldon for allowing me to utilize some of the language of his book as I drafted this book for my Michigan readers. By doing so, it allowed me to expedite completion of this consumer book as the effective date of July 1, 2020 fast approached.

With knowledge comes power, the power to help yourself and others. I'm not in the business of selling auto insurance nor do I recommend buying auto insurance from any particular insurance company. That said, I am an experienced motor vehicle accident attorney. The message I "sell" is for you, the consumer, to "buy" protection for you and your family from being victimized by being involved in a serious motor vehicle accident. For over 30 years, I have helped accident victims and their families who, through no fault of their own, were seriously injured or had loved ones killed in a motor vehicle accident.

It may, therefore, seem confusing to some readers why I, as a Michigan motor vehicle accident attorney, and not as an insurance salesman, frequently speak and write about purchasing proper insurance coverage in Michigan. Let me explain:

- In short, **if** the money (insurance) isn't there on a client's (victim's) part, or **on** the part of the at-fault party, there just isn't any money to compensate for:

    - The expenses of excess medical care (past and future)

    - The loss of income (past and future)

    - An individual's loss of social pleasures in life

    - The loss of an individual's financial ability to support themselves and family members for life

    - An individual's pain and suffering (past and future)

- Hiring individuals to perform household services that the injured party was able to perform for themselves before being injured

- Property damage done to your vehicle (up to $3,000)

• All of the above are recoverable "damages" for an injured party in a motor vehicle accident, but only if there is adequate insurance coverage to pay for such losses.

• A person without adequate insurance coverage is often just plain out of luck – *no matter how skilled or talented the lawyer they hire to represent them!*

I wrote this book because I strongly believe that public education is the first step in helping you, the consumer, to be in a better position to recover from a motor vehicle accident. **My message to you is: Make sure you adequately protect yourself before you ever get into a motor vehicle accident.**

A person without adequate insurance coverage is often just plain out of luck – *no matter how skilled or talented the lawyer they hire to represent them!*

CHAPTER TWO

"BUT, I THOUGHT I HAD 'FULL COVERAGE'?"

This is one of the most common statements heard from motor vehicle accident victims coming into my office seeking help. Unfortunately, many of them find out that they only purchased an insurance policy that provides for the minimum coverage necessary to legally drive in Michigan. Sadly, this is by no means "full or even adequate insurance coverage." People are amazed and shocked when they receive this heartbreaking news. This is why it is so important that you be informed regarding the pitfalls of purchasing inadequate coverage under Michigan's "new" No-Fault motor vehicle laws.

1. Since October of 1973, Michigan required <u>every driver</u> to purchase unlimited medical-related expense coverage under

Section 3107(1)(a) of Michigan's No-Fault Law. Previously, all reasonable and necessary medical-related expenses for the injured party were covered for life. Such expenses covered ongoing treatment for the symptoms arising out of the injured party's injuries, such as chiropractic treatment, massage treatment, physical therapy, psychological counseling, construction of ramps for wheelchair bound individuals, ambulance costs (which could amount to thousands of dollars for an air-vac transport), and many more medical-related expenses **other than just hospital bills and doctor visits.**

2. Beginning on July 1, 2020, Michigan citizens will be required to select from many options available to them, many of which will provide limitations on the medical expenses and coverages available to them all in the name of "saving money." Michigan citizens will only be able to save money, if at all, by limiting their coverages for medical-related expenses by choosing to "opt out" of unlimited medical coverage that they previously had under Michigan's *old* No-Fault Law. Michigan citizens will be given options to decrease unlimited coverage and instead opt to limit their medical-related expenses to $500,000, $250,000, $50,000, or no coverage at all if they have Medicare coverage available to them.

3. By way of analogy, if an individual had an insurance policy providing $1 million for their loved ones should they die, which cost $3,000/year in premiums, such an individual could "save" premium costs by simply "opting

out" of having $1 million of coverage and paying for less coverage. If that individual dropped their life insurance coverage to $750,000, they could reduce their annual insurance premium to $2,500. If they dropped it further to $500,000 or $250,000, they could "save even more money" by reducing their annual insurance premium to $2,000 or $1,500 a year. And, if they opted to only have $100,000 or $50,000 of life insurance coverage, they could "save even more" and reduce their annual premium to $1,000/year or $500/year. Hopefully, this analogy makes the picture clear. Yes, Michigan motorists can "save money" if they choose to *decrease* their current coverage available to them, which they would otherwise have if they continued to pay for unlimited coverage for all medical-related expenses under MCL 500.3107(1)(a).

4. It's extremely important to realize that Michigan's No-Fault Law requires insurance companies to pay for many benefits that a simple healthcare policy or Medicare coverage will not cover for injuries sustained in an auto accident.

All of these related expenses are mandatory for reimbursement to the injured parties under MCL 500.3107(1)(a) to help seriously injured individuals in motor vehicle accidents return, as much as possible, to their normal life after incurring life-altering injuries from a motor vehicle accident.

CHAPTER THREE

MY SIMPLE 3-STEP APPROACH TO BUYING AUTO INSURANCE

STEP 1. DO YOUR HOMEWORK:

Start educating yourself about the various auto insurance coverages available by <u>reading this book</u> and then doing your own individual research.

- This book will provide basic information which is necessary to help you ask the right questions.

- Armed with the educational foundation that you receive from this book, you will then be in a position to evaluate insurance agents and determine if they are knowledgeable and whether they will be there when and if you need them should you become involved in an auto accident.

- You can also check websites, such as: www.michigan.gov/autoinsurance.

STEP 2. GET EXPERT ADVICE:

Once you have a basic education, visit a reputable, experienced **local** insurance agent in your community for guidance. He or she can recommend the amount and types of coverage you need to protect yourself and your family.

- I recommend finding a local agent who represents a major company that is financially strong and has a reputation for treating policy holders fairly.

- Or find a well-respected independent agent who will compare rates and coverage among several insurance companies.

- This wise advice is free.

- Online or phone consult insurance companies are NOT the best place to seek expert advice regarding your individual Michigan auto insurance needs!

STEP 3. SHOP PRICE.

Once you determine your insurance needs, begin competitive pricing the costs of the best coverage for you and your family that you believe you can afford.

BOTTOM LINE RECOMMENDATIONS

- If you choose to buy online or by phone, make sure you know what you need before you contact them! Often, a "price-oriented" salesperson makes a sale based on price alone. These companies may have inexperienced customer service representatives who do not know how to adequately evaluate you and your family's Michigan auto insurance needs.

- **I recommend buying your insurance through a local, reputable insurance agent.** Local insurance agents live in your neighborhood and are part of the mosaic of your community. They raise their families, go to church, attend PTA meetings, and donate to local causes. Chances are, local agents have cultivated relationships with the local claim's office, so that when it comes time to help you with a sticky situation on a claim, they can become your advocate.

- Local agents can recommend body shops, towing services, glass replacement facilities, and when necessary, a good, local motor vehicle accident attorney.

- While saving money is always a factor, don't forget that every time you ride in a motor vehicle, you are placing yourself at the mercy of other drivers. With that in mind, you need to protect yourself and your loved ones, as both your life and their lives could easily be altered forever by someone else's negligence.

CHAPTER FOUR

UNDERSTANDING INSURANCE TERMS AND "WHAT KINDS OF LOSSES" AUTO INSURANCE COVERS

In every motor vehicle accident, the **first party** is **your** insurance company or the insurance company, under priority rules, responsible for paying **your** Personal Injury Protection benefits. These benefits provided to you are collectively referred to as your PIP benefits. To register a motor vehicle, every Michigan motor vehicle owner is required, by law, to purchase first party PIP benefits. PIP benefits provide money for such things as:

- **Work loss** for the first three years after the accident;

- Reimbursement for **replacement services** (hiring people to do things for you that you were previously able to do but can no longer perform due to accident-related

BUYING AUTO INSURANCE IN MICHIGAN

injuries). These replacement services include lawn care, childcare, snow shoveling, grocery shopping, and household chores. Reimbursement for the costs of replacement services is available for up to three years after the accident;

- Reimbursement for **medical-related expenses <u>for life</u>** (up to any expense cap you select under the new No-Fault laws unless you completely opt-out of such coverage with the Medicare opt-out option), and

- Reimbursement for **home attendant care** (up to either 8 hours a day or potentially up to 24 hours a day).

PIP benefits are available <u>regardless</u> of whether the injured party was at-fault for causing the accident. That is part of the reason why Michigan's Motor Vehicle Insurance law is referred to as "No-Fault Insurance."

In every motor vehicle accident where an individual has been injured or killed, the injured party or the decedent's estate is referred to as the **second party**. If the **second party** was injured or killed as the result of the negligence of another, then another person, the "at-fault party" and his or her insurance company are collectively referred to as the **third party**. Obviously, if the injured or deceased party was involved in a single vehicle accident (e.g., the driver fell asleep, ran off the road and hit a tree), then there is no **third party**. So, briefly:

1. **First party**: refers to the insurance company providing PIP benefits, typically your own insurance company.

2. **Second party**: refers to the injured person or deceased person's estate.

3. **Third party**: refers to the person at-fault, and his or her insurance company.

CHAPTER FIVE

THERE ARE ONLY 3 REQUIRED AUTO INSURANCE COVERAGES IN MICHIGAN

1. **Coverage for an injured individual's personal injury protection benefits (PIP benefits) and their medical-related expenses.** Individuals will have to select coverages which may limit their medical-related expenses coverage under MCL 500.3107(1)(a) to a "capped" sum, less than the existing unlimited coverage, or individuals may elect to opt out entirely from any PIP coverage and choose instead to rely on whatever Medicare coverage provides, if they are eligible to qualify for Medicare.

    As will be discussed later in this book, to save premium costs, many individuals will opt to go with caps on their coverage limits for their medical-related expenses, capping such costs at $500,000, $250,000 or $50,000. These selections to decrease medical-related expense coverage will all be selected now to reduce annual premiums for motor vehicle insurance coverage and done simply "to save money."

The PIP "opt-outs" could also eliminate wage loss coverage.

It needs to be kept in mind that $50,000 of medical-related expenses can be used up before an injured party even gets out of the emergency room. Ultimately, selecting lower caps on coverage for medical-related expenses will shift the responsibility for paying for an injured party's medical expenses to the at-fault driver who caused an accident (a reason why Michigan motorists need to consider purchasing umbrella policies to protect themselves). If the at-fault driver has no significant auto insurance themselves, an individual will either be forced to go on public assistance and receive coverage through Medicaid, file for bankruptcy or both. Any options to seek medical-related expense coverage from an at-fault driver, however, obviously will not exist when a Michigan driver caused the accident resulting in their own injuries.

2. **Third party bodily injury liability insurance coverage.** Previously, under Michigan's *old* No-Fault Law, the minimum limits for bodily injury were $20,000 per individual/$40,000 per accident, regardless of how many individuals were injured. As of July 1, 2020, all Michigan drivers must carry at least a $50,000 BI coverage for any one individual injured in an accident or $100,000 coverage for all individuals who may be injured in a motor vehicle

accident. If two individuals are injured, then one individual can get up to $50,000 while the other individual will have that same option (i.e., one individual cannot receive $75,000 and the other $25,000). That doesn't mean that each individual will actually receive $50,000 each, but that is the maximum each individual is required to have coverage for under Michigan's new No-Fault laws. If 4 people are injured and each one was injured seriously (i.e., 4 people were killed, then the $100,000 of coverage would likely be divided with $25,000 being offered to each of the 4 individuals' estates).

Under Michigan's new No-Fault laws, a default provision requires auto insurance agents to recommend to each purchaser of bodily injury coverage a policy of insurance of at least $250,000 per individual and $500,000 for each accident (for all injured parties). That said, individuals are not required to purchase this level of coverage and may "opt-out" for lesser coverage going all the way down to $50,000 per individual and $100,000 per accident. Insurance companies will likely also offer lesser amounts of coverage between the $50,000 per individual and $100,000 per accident and the recommended $250,000 per individual and $500,000 per accident such as $100,000/$300,000.

RECOMMENDATIONS FOR BODILY INJURY COVERAGE:

I recommend Bodily Injury coverage in the amount of $250,000 per individual and $500,000 per accident <u>as a minimum</u> for every Michigan consumer. Personally, I recommend a higher coverage of $500,000 per accident and $1,000,000 if it is made available to you at affordable costs to better protect individuals you might accidentally injure. There are other options such as $500,000 per accident that should also be considered. If you have substantial assets, a higher amount is recommended, as well as purchasing an Umbrella/Excess policy for a minimum of $1,000,000. Individuals with more significant financial assets should consider $2,000,000 Umbrellas or $5,000,000 Umbrellas, if made available to them.

Typically, you can only purchase Uninsured Motorist (UM) coverage or Underinsured Motorist coverage up to the amount of your Bodily Injury policy. Accordingly, the higher your Bodily Injury policy, the higher UM coverage you are able to purchase.

3. **Property damage** coverage to protect you if your motor vehicle causes damage to another individual's property (other than another motor vehicle being driven and involved in the accident). All Michigan drivers are required to carry $1 million for property damage. While Michigan drivers are required to carry $1 million in coverage for property damage, in most other states the minimum property damage requirement is much lower, typically $10,000. A Michigan car insurance policy may list the minimum property damage limit at being $10,000, but such $10,000 limit only applies to out-of-state claims. Accordingly, if you are a Michigan resident and frequently drive out of state, you may wish to increase your minimum property damage limit for out of state accidents so that you can be certain

to have enough coverage. This is something to talk to your local insurance agent about when you purchase your auto insurance. Any property damage which occurs in the State of Michigan is covered under a separate coverage called Property Protection Insurance (PPI).

Under Michigan's new No-Fault laws, a default provision requires auto insurance agents to recommend to each purchaser of bodily injury coverage a policy of insurance of at least $250,000 per individual and $500,000 for each accident (for all injured parties).

CHAPTER SIX

OTHER FORMS OF IMPORTANT INSURANCE COVERAGES AVAILABLE IN MICHIGAN

UM Coverage

UM coverage covers 2 different types of situations., The first is when the motor vehicle accident involves a collision with another vehicle whose driver was uninsured, meaning he/she had no insurance at all covering the vehicle being driven by him/her at the time of colliding with your vehicle.

The second type of situation is when the individual driving the vehicle that collided with your vehicle had some form of insurance but the coverage for bodily injury was minimal, in light of the injuries sustained by you or occupants of your vehicle.

Obviously, in the second situation, the other motorist will typically be a Michigan resident, but trust me, many accidents occur where the other driver is either a Canadian citizen or an out-of-state resident. Often times bodily injury requirements may be as low as $10,000 per accident and if you or your loved ones are seriously injured, $10,000 doesn't go far when it comes to compensating you or family members for serious injuries.

Later in this book, under the section Understanding Insurance Terms and What Kind of Losses Auto Insurance Covers, I will go into much greater depth with my recommendations regarding purchasing UM coverage.

Limited property damage coverage/also known as "mini tort coverage."

Mini tort coverage protects you when you cause damage to another party's motor vehicle that is not otherwise covered by the other party's insurance. Such coverage has increased from $1,000 under the other No-Fault laws per motor vehicle to $3,000 per motor vehicle under Michigan's new No-Fault laws, effective July 1, 2020. The language in the new No-Fault laws states, "to the extent that the damages done to your own vehicle are not covered by your insurance, you are covered if an at-fault driver caused the damage to your motor vehicle."

In the event that a Michigan driver's vehicle is damaged and another insured driver was at-fault for causing the accident, the other driver is liable for collision damages up to $3,000. **If your vehicle has a deductible that does not cover your vehicle damage for the first $1,000, $2,000 or $3,000, as the case may be, you may receive compensation for uncovered**

damage done to your vehicle (up to $3,000) if the other driver was at-fault. Typically, the at-fault driver, if insured, will have coverage for this type of claim and such coverage is referred to as mini tort coverage. If there is any issue as to who was at fault, comparative negligence is relevant up to 50% and such a request for reimbursement might end up having to be litigated in small claims court.

CHAPTER SEVEN

PROTECTING DAMAGE TO YOUR OWN VEHICLE

There are 2 other important types of coverages which are available, though not mandatory to protect damage done to your own motor vehicle, and they should always be considered. The **first** is called **comprehensive coverage**. This type of coverage is distinguished from collision coverage in the sense that it typically protects your vehicle from damage caused by forces other than being involved in a motor vehicle accident. It is distinguished from collision coverage, which **does** cover your vehicle when it is being driven and collides with another vehicle, or while being driven, collides with other objects such as trees, buildings, etc.

Comprehensive insurance typically covers damage done to your vehicle while your vehicle is being stored. Such damage could occur as a result of a fire, weather related causes (wind could blow over a tree causing it to fall on your vehicle, or fall on the building in which your vehicle is being stored, i.e., or your garage), flooding, damages from rodents entering your vehicle, windshield damage caused by outside forces, theft of your vehicle, and vandalism done to your vehicle by other individuals. Comprehensive insurance can also cover damage to your vehicle when it is hit by an animal, such as a deer or a bird. If you have broad collision and comprehensive, typically the auto insurance company will waive your deductible. If you just have just comprehensive coverage, then typically a deductible will apply.

The **second** form of coverage to protect your vehicle, is referred to as **collision coverage**. It needs to be noted that some insurance companies will not sell a consumer collision coverage without the consumer also purchasing comprehensive insurance. That said, other insurance companies will allow the consumer to purchase collision coverage without the consumer also purchasing comprehensive coverage. Collision coverage provides reimbursement for damage done to your vehicle, or replacement of your vehicle, if it's damaged beyond repair (i.e., your vehicle was "totaled"). Accordingly, collision coverage will repair damages done to your vehicle or refund you the actual cash value of your vehicle, if it is damaged beyond repair, Again, that collision could take place with either another vehicle or an inanimate object such as a fence, a tree, or a building. While collision coverage is not mandatory in Michigan, it may become "mandatory" if you take out a loan to purchase your vehicle, since the lending financial institution will typically require you to purchase such collision coverage.

This only makes sense, since the good condition of your motor vehicle is the collateral for the financial institution's loan to you, and the financial institution's lien presumes that it is attaching to an undamaged vehicle.

Again, collision coverage does extend beyond just motor vehicle accidents and covers damage done to your vehicle for things like running over a pothole, hitting a guardrail, etc. Once again, if your vehicle is totaled, there may be a dispute as to the actual cash value of your car at the time of the damage being inflicted. Previous repairs could reduce the value of your car. If you keep photographs showing the good condition of your vehicle, they can help you should there come a time to resolve an issue of your vehicle's "actual cash value." Make sure to discuss with your insurance agent the different types of collision coverage available to you.

Terms like **broad collision**, which is typically the best and the most expensive coverage you can purchase, will allow you to have your vehicle repaired without any deductible if you are not at-fault in causing the damage to your vehicle. This type of coverage is very good for you to have, especially in the case where your vehicle was a parked vehicle and you don't know who caused the damage. Under broad collision coverage, you would be able to get your vehicle repaired without paying any deductible. On the other hand, if you are an at-fault driver and caused the accident, you will be required to pay the deductible listed on your collision coverage.

Other types of collision coverage include what is known as the **standard or regular collision** and it is less expensive. In this type of coverage, regardless of fault, you will be required to pay your deductible when repairing damage done to your vehicle (or replacing your vehicle if it was totaled). If another driver caused the damage to your vehicle, under Michigan's new No-Fault laws, it will be possible to make a claim for up to $3,000 from the at-fault driver's insurance policy, called a mini tort claim, if the other driver had such mini tort coverage in effect at the time of the collision. If the at-fault driver had insurance coverage, but did not have mini tort coverage, then you could still sue the at-fault driver in small claims court for damage to your vehicle up to $3,000. If you did not have collision coverage and if the at-fault driver did not have no-fault insurance coverage, you could sue the at-fault driver for the total value of the damage done to your vehicle.

Lastly, **limited collision** is typically the least expensive form of collision coverage. With limited collision coverage, you will only be covered if the accident that damaged your vehicle was not your fault. In this scenario, typically no deductible will apply, but it needs to be kept in mind that if you were at fault causing the accident, you will not have any coverage provided by your limited collision selection.

If your vehicle is totaled, there may be a dispute as to the actual cash value of your car at the time of the damage being inflicted. Previous repairs could reduce the value of your car.

CHAPTER EIGHT

FACTS/STATISTICS REGARDING MICHIGAN'S UNINSURED/ UNDERINSURED DRIVERS

Considering the following facts/statistics, it becomes clear why having adequate insurance coverage is vitally important in Michigan and uninsured/underinsured motorist coverage is so valuable.

Driver's on the road in Michigan:

- According to the Insurance Research Council (IRC), 21.3%, or 1 out of about every 5 drivers in Michigan.... are <u>uninsured</u>, driving without any insurance, and are driving illegally. Michigan ranks fourth in the Nation for the number of insured drivers.

•   Add to those statistics the fact that a significant percentage of Michigan drivers will have only the required minimum insurance ($50,000), which offers you <u>very little protection</u> for your excess medical bills (over any cap you select), lost wages, and other out-of-pocket expenses in excess of what coverage you purchased. Those individuals are "underinsured" when it comes to protecting you for the losses you could sustain in a motor vehicle accident.

Summary

Accordingly, I estimate that approximately 50% of Michigan driver's (**1 out of 2 drivers!**) have no or only a limited amount of insurance coverage available to cover your excess hospital bills and medical expenses, rehabilitation costs, excess loss of wages, disability, loss of social pleasures, pain and suffering, mental anguish, etc. if you are injured in a motor vehicle accident.

CHAPTER NINE

HOW TO PURCHASE ADEQUATE MICHIGAN AUTO INSURANCE AT A COMPETITIVE PRICE

What can you do about this? It's simple, protect yourself and your family by **you** purchasing adequate auto insurance! Here are my recommendations about how best to go about doing so:

<u>First</u>, understand that there are many different types of insurance coverages available to purchase.

<u>Second</u>, making matter worse, consumers are bombarded with TV ads offering low cost insurance if we just call or go online. It is hard to know what to do and how to make sense of it all.

Third, it is difficult to find good information about the many insurance products because some agents either just want to sell insurance or do not have the knowledge and understanding of the coverages available, especially under Michigan's new No-Fault laws.

Fourth, with Michigan's new PIP coverage options, it's more important than ever that the consumer understand the implications of selecting less than unlimited PIP coverage, especially as the same relates to reimbursement for medical-related expenses.

There are "opt-outs" for coverages for medical-related expenses, work loss, and potentially attendant care. Again, the key to all of these "opt-outs" is that the consumer will receive **reduced benefits** that would otherwise be available to them should they be seriously injured in a motor vehicle accident.

CHAPTER TEN

INSURANCE COVERAGES AVAILABLE TO PAY FOR AN INJURED PARTY'S LOSSES

PIP Benefits

These benefits are referred to as First Party benefits and typically come from the insurance company that **you** purchased your insurance coverage from to protect you and your household family members if you are injured in a motor vehicle accident, regardless of fault (i.e., even if the accident occurred as a result of **your** fault). These benefits are also available to you from your own insurance company if someone else was at-fault for causing the accident.

By law, these benefits reimburse you for your **medical-related expenses** (up to the cap of such expenses you select from

Michigan's new No-Fault options, unless you opt out of such coverage with the Medicare opt-out option). These benefits also reimburse you for **wage loss** for the first three years after your accident, **replacement services**, for hiring someone to help perform tasks that you can no longer perform for yourself, and for **survivor losses** when there has been a death of a person responsible for providing eligible dependents.

Excess Economic Losses

Such excess economic losses can be recovered against an at-fault driver when the injured party was earning more than the statutory monthly wage maximum ($5,718 per month in 2020), or the injured party will likely be unable to continue with his or her pre-accident employment in the future beyond three years after the accident date. This occurrence is typically referred to as a future wage loss.

In a future wage loss situation, persons in their 30s could be earning $50,000 per year and supporting a spouse and minor children and receive serious injuries preventing such a worker from being able to work for the rest of their lives. You only have to "do the math" to realize how costly this could be to the injured party and his/her dependents. As an example, let's say the injured party was 32 years of age when injured or killed in a motor vehicle accident that was someone else's fault. By age 35, a future wage loss (three years after the accident) would commence and continue for the anticipated work life of that individual per economic tables. If we just assumed that they would have worked to age 65, that's 30 years times $50,000 per year in wage loss, or a $1,500,000 loss! Even when reducing this figure by 15% for taxes on likely future income, and further reducing such a loss to present day value, you have a present-day future wage loss to the individual and his/her dependents in the range of $1,000,000!

If the individual was earning in excess of the statutory monthly minimum ($5,718 in 2020), the injured party would also have an excess economic loss for the first three years after the accident. A claim could be maintained against the at-fault driver (or his or her insurance company) for the difference in his/her economic loss not covered by his own insurance company's PIP benefits for wage loss for the first three years after the accident.

Non-economic Losses

These losses are allowed to be recovered from an at-fault driver, or from your own UM coverage if the at-fault driver had no insurance (as in the case of a hit and run situation), or if the at-fault driver had inadequate insurance coverage to fully compensate the seriously injured party or the deceased party's estate (i.e., the at-fault driver had the statutory minimum bodily coverage of $50,000 per individual or even a $100,000 or a $250,000 bodily coverage maximum, as the case might be in the case of a catastrophic injury).

These allowable losses that the injured party could be compensated for include the injured party's:

1. Physical pain and suffering

2. Mental anguish

3. Fright and shock

4. Denial of social pleasure and enjoyments of life

5. Embarrassment, humiliation or mortification as a result of their injuries.

6. Disability and disfigurement.

Non-economic losses may be allowed for the future if there is a likelihood that such losses will continue to be sustained by the injured party.

Picture yourself receiving a catastrophic life-altering injury. You lose a leg or become a quadriplegic. You had a life expectancy of 50 years to live before the accident, and you were supporting a spouse and minor children before being catastrophically injured. Is a one-time payment of $50,000 or $100,000 enough compensation to fully and fairly compensate you for 50 or more years of a life of misery, pain and for your loss of social pleasures like going for walks, bicycling, boating, going hunting, going skiing and enjoying yourself at the beach? Clearly, $50,000 or $100,000 is like a drop of water in a large bucket when it comes to compensating you for all of what was inflicted upon you and taken away from you by the carelessness of an at-fault driver.

CHAPTER ELEVEN

PURCHASING UM COVERAGE

How do you protect yourself and your family members from the impact of being seriously injured in a motor vehicle accident?

The answer is simple. You need to purchase a high amount of what is collectively referred to as **UM Coverage**. Since you purchase this type of coverage yourself, it's generally classified under First Party Coverage (your own insurance company), but it's only available to protect you if you or a family member are injured <u>as a result of another at-fault driver</u> who had no insurance coverage or only had a low amount of insurance coverage.

Many insurance companies separate these two types of coverages into separate coverages. <u>Uninsurance coverage</u> applies in situations where the at-fault driver had **no** insurance, while <u>underinsurance coverage</u> comes into play when the at-fault driver had insurance coverage but with **low bodily injury limits** which, when contrasted with your serious injuries, are deemed to be inadequate to fully and fairly compensate you, the injured party. Both of these coverages should be purchased by the Michigan consumer to best protect themselves and their family members from the fallout of being seriously injured in a motor vehicle accident.

1. **Uninsurance coverage.** The limits you purchase, $100,000, $250,000, $500,000 or $1,000,000, if available, would then provide coverage to you or a family member, for excess economic losses or to compensate you for your non-economic losses (pain, suffering, loss of social pleasures in life, etc.) when the at-fault driver has no bodily injury coverage.

2. **Underinsurance coverage.** The limits of coverage you can purchase for this type of coverage are typically the same as you purchase to protect you for causing injuries to others, and that is $100,000, $250,000, $500,000 or $1,000,000. The amount of coverage you purchase must exceed Michigan Minimum Bodily Injury coverage of $50,000 per individual. This coverage compensates you or injured members of your household for excess economic losses or for non-economic losses (pain, suffering, loss of social pleasures, etc.) when the at-fault driver had bodily injury insurance coverage, but not enough insurance coverage to adequately compensate you for your losses (i.e., $50,000, $250,000, or even $500,000 in the case of a catastrophic

injury). These higher amounts of bodily injury insurance coverage would be necessary to fully and fairly compensate you or a family member who has been seriously injured from a motor vehicle accident. Again, if injuries to you have forever altered your life (i.e., loss of a limb, a neurological injury, any type of injury preventing you from being able to continue to be gainfully employed), then $50,000 of bodily injury insurance coverage coming from the at-fault driver's insurance company is simply not enough to fairly compensate you for your excess economic losses and your non-economic damages (pain and suffering, loss of social pleasures of life, etc.).

Underinsurance coverage <u>can make up the difference</u>. If you purchased a $500,000 underinsurance policy, and are catastrophically injured or die, and the at-fault driver had $50,000 of bodily injury coverage, your underinsurance coverage of $500,000 would make up the difference by writing you or your family member a check for $450,000. You are buying protection for you and a family member who has been seriously injured as a result of a motor vehicle driver's negligence, when the other driver was "under insured" to provide bodily insurance coverage for your excess economic losses and non-economic losses sustained by you or a family or a household member.

In my opinion, purchasing a large amount of underinsurance coverage can be the most important coverage you purchase to protect yourself or a family/household member from the tragedies of being seriously injured in a motor vehicle accident. Accordingly, be sure to discuss purchasing <u>a high amount of coverage</u> for this type of insurance, underinsured coverage. The good news is that the annual increase in premium cost for purchasing a large amount of underinsurance is not that expensive (perhaps as little as $50-$75 per year) and well worth securing the peace of mind that such coverage brings from protecting yourself and your loved ones.

In my opinion, purchasing a large amount of underinsurance coverage can be the most important coverage you purchase to protect yourself or a family/household member from the tragedies of being seriously injured in a motor vehicle accident.

CHAPTER TWELVE

WARNING: BE AWARE OF INTRA-FAMILY EXCLUSIONARY CLAUSES
-A/K/A STEP-DOWN CLAUSES

A step-down insurance clause or intra-family exclusionary clause basically says that any person unrelated to the insured, who is injured while riding in the insured's vehicle, gets **more** coverage than an insured's own family member who also may be injured in the same crash. Depending on the language, a Michigan auto insurance policy might insert a clause stating, "Coverage under part II, including our duty to defend, will **NOT** apply to any injured person for…bodily injury to you or a relative. This exclusion applies only to damages in excess of the minimum limit mandated by the Motor Vehicle Financial Responsibility Law of Michigan" ($50,000/$100,000 effective July 1, 2020). The bottom line is this, Michigan auto insurance policies that include a step-down clause, treat the insured's own family members harsher than complete strangers!!!

Sadly, most Michigan residents don't even know that this limiting language has been inserted into their auto insurance policy. How can this possibly occur? Insurance companies don't say anything about it, and insurance agents may not even know it's in the policy that they are selling because it's standard for certain insurance carriers to include such provisions. Sadly, as a Michigan motor vehicle accident attorney, I see these clauses all the time and, unfortunately, they often times seriously diminish your family member's recoverable compensation. From my perspective, these family step-down clauses are repugnant and reprehensible.

I continue to be amazed that Michigan's Insurance Commissioner allows these clauses to be inserted in Michigan Motorist No-Fault Insurance policies. Before you purchase a policy, **make sure that there are no intra-family exclusionary clauses or step-down clauses included.** If there is such a clause, my simple advice is, **DON'T BUY SUCH AN INSURANCE POLICY!**

Recently I represented a family member whose wife was killed in a motor vehicle accident. His son was the at-fault driver who went through a stop sign. Another son riding in the vehicle was also seriously injured and will likely never fully recover from his injuries. Even though for over 20 years he had paid for $100,000/$300,000 coverage, under the step-down provision, both he, as the survivor of his deceased wife, and his son, were limited to Michigan's minimum insurance coverage of $20,000 per individual. What a tragedy! He had absolutely no idea that this step-down provision was included in his insurance policy.

> *Before you purchase a policy, make sure that there are no intra-family exclusionary clauses or step-down clauses included.*

CHAPTER THIRTEEN

PERSONAL INJURY PROTECTION (PIP) BENEFITS
- UNDERSTANDING WHAT IS INCLUDED

It needs to be kept in mind that the greater part of an individual's insurance premium cost covers what is known as first party personal injury protection benefits (PIP Benefits). PIP benefits protect the individual who is paying the insurance premium. Stated another way, the high cost of motor vehicle insurance occurs typically as a result of benefits that are paid to the injured individual who paid for the insurance coverages. The primary reason for the high cost of motor vehicle insurance for PIP coverage is due to the high cost of medical care and the high cost of replacing incomes that are lost when injured parties are unable to continue in their employment.

PIP benefits are available for the occupants in the insured's motor vehicle, and for individuals who are injured by the operation of a motor vehicle (example: a pedestrian, a bicyclist, or a motorcyclist, irrespective of who was at fault for causing the injury or injuries).

Buying protection for a motor vehicle accident for PIP benefits is similar to buying health insurance or life insurance. It's a social program designed to spread the risk of doing an inherently dangerous act, to wit: driving a motor vehicle, even when no other driver contributes to causing an accident.

WHOSE INSURANCE COMPANY PAYS PIP BENEFITS?

- PIP benefits are typically paid by your own insurance company, <u>regardless of who was at fault in causing an accident</u>. There are cases where pedestrians, bicyclists and motorcycle riders are injured where an insurance company other than a policy purchased by the injured party may be required to provide PIP benefits.

WHO IS COVERED BY PIP BENEFITS?

- You, the insured, are covered by PIP benefits while driving your motor vehicle, or when riding as a passenger in another vehicle, or if you are walking (a pedestrian) or biking and are struck by a motor vehicle.

- Children and relatives who live in your household may also be covered while driving your car, riding as a passenger in your or another's car, or if they are walking (a pedestrian) or biking and are struck by a motor vehicle.

• Others who drive your insured motor vehicle or are injured while riding as a passenger in your car, may also be covered by your PIP benefits.

• PIP benefits may be paid even if a motor vehicle accident occurs outside of the State of Michigan, as long as you are injured while driving in your insured vehicle in the United States, its territories, its possessions or Canada.

PIP exclusions and exceptions:

• PIP does not cover drivers or riders of motorcycles, unless they are injured by another motor vehicle.

• The insurance company may exclude PIP benefits for injury to any person operating the vehicle without the owner's express or implied consent.

• PIP benefits will be excluded if the driver caused or contributed to the injury intentionally or while committing a felony.

• PIP coverage may not cover drivers specifically excluded by the insurance policy or not disclosed to the insurance company (usually other household members).

IS PIP COVERAGE REQUIRED IN MICHIGAN?

Yes. Michigan law requires vehicle owners to carry some form of PIP coverage.

WHAT ARE THE TYPICAL TYPES OF PIP BENEFITS?

Generally speaking, the 4 types of PIP benefits available under Michigan's No-Fault law are as follows:

1. **Reimbursement for reasonable charges incurred in paying for necessary products, services, and accommodations for an injured person's care, recovery, or rehabilitation.** Under Section 3107(1)(a), many services and products are available to be reimbursed by auto insurance coverage that are not typically reimbursable by Medicare or healthcare policies. When individuals who have opted-out of receiving reimbursement for medical-related expenses, choosing to rely strictly on Medicare, in addition to having many services not covered they may have deductibles or co-pays that they cannot afford.

2. **Wage loss benefits.** These benefits are payable for up to 3 years after a motor vehicle accident and are typically calculated at 85% of the individual's gross income that they were receiving prior to the accident, or would have received, had the individual not been injured and disabled. There is a monthly cap involved in this benefit.

3. **Reimbursement for replacement service expenses**. This reimbursement is payable again, for up to 3 years and consists of a $20/day reimbursement to the injured person when he or she is required to hire other individuals to perform services that they used to perform for themselves.

Types of Replacement Services:

Some examples of replacement services that can be reimbursed include:

- Household cleaning (vacuuming, dusting, washing floors, taking out the trash, changing the linen on beds, cleaning bathrooms, etc.)

- Doing laundry (folding clothes, ironing, putting clothes away, etc.)

- Performing lawn care functions (mowing the grass, raking leaves, weeding, trimming hedges, etc.)

- Grocery shopping and shopping for children's clothes

- Snow shoveling

- Providing for childcare

- Making household repairs

- Making vehicle repairs (changing oil, etc.)

- Preparing meals

- Bathing family members and caring for the physical needs of other family members

NOTE: *Expenses for obtaining replacement services must be reasonably incurred. Court decisions have recognized that a simple, oral agreement, or even an implied agreement between family members that they will be compensated is enough. Spouses, children, and parents of an injured party are the norm, rather than the exception, to perform such replacement services. Don't be timid when asking for reimbursement for these expenses. Remember that **you** paid for these benefits every time you paid your insurance premiums.*

4. **Survivor's Loss Benefits.** These benefits are payable for 3 years to the dependents of the deceased individual who was insured. These benefits cover several different types of losses including funeral expenses, lost wages, and replacement services, etc.

WHO PAYS PIP BENEFITS TO AN INDIVIDUAL INJURED OR KILLED IN A MOTOR VEHICLE ACCIDENT?

Typically, an injured person needs to turn to his or her own auto No-Fault insurance company. That said, there are a number of exceptions, such as individuals who are riding on motorcycles, or riding in or driving an employer provided vehicle, or for persons who do not have No-Fault insurance who may be involved in a motor vehicle accident, such as being injured as a pedestrian or as a bicyclist.

WHAT ARE THE TIME LIMITS FOR SEEKING PIP BENEFITS?

A person who incurs expenses or would otherwise be eligible for normal No-Fault PIP benefits (work loss, replacement services, etc.), must submit written notice to their responsible insurance company within 1 year of the date of the accident (BEWARE, some policies even require a 6 month notice) and must include the specific information required by the No-Fault Act. Additionally, once a claim is submitted to the No-Fault Insurance carrier, if it is not paid within 30 days, a legal action must be filed within 1 year of the date that the particular expense was incurred or that right to enforce payment will be barred by a statutory limitation.

WHAT ABOUT NO-FAULT PIP BENEFITS BEING REDUCED BY OTHER BENEFITS BEING RECEIVED BY THE INJURED PARTY?

Depending on whether the policy that you purchase is an uncoordinated or an excluder or coordinated No-Fault policy, No-Fault benefits could be reduced by the amounts other health insurers would pay on your behalf, should you become injured. Also, there are cases where offsets are made because government benefits may be payable, as when injured individuals begin receiving Social Security Disability payments.

UNDER MICHIGAN'S NEW NO-FAULT LAW, WHAT TYPE OF OPTIONS ARE AVAILABLE WHEN IT COMES TO SELECTING PIP BENEFITS?

Michigan's Legislature passed the new No-Fault laws which were signed into law on June 11, 2019 by Governor Gretchen Whitmer. The managed care option of the new No-Fault law was given immediate effect with the remainder of the options under Personal Injury Protection Benefits going into effect July 1, 2020.

All types of different PIP coverage options are now available to Michigan citizens when they purchase their insurance coverage. Formerly, if an individual was injured in a motor vehicle accident, their medical-related expenses, under Section 3107(1)(a), were covered for life and extended to cover many related rehabilitation expenses outside of actual healthcare expenses.

Medically-Related Expenses:

Some examples of the medical care and reasonable rehabilitation services that PIP benefits cover include:

- Job training and job placement services/Vocational rehabilitation

- Cognitive therapy/Speech therapy/Psychotherapy

- Doctor visits/Chiropractic visits

- Hospitalizations

- X-rays, MRI's, CT-Scans, Digital Motion X-rays

- Physical therapy treatment

- Surgeries

- Prescription medications

- Counseling

Attendant Care:

Additionally, in-home attendant care services can be provided to the victim by outside agencies or by a nurse or a family member. Attendant care services may involve:

- Bathing

- Dressing

- Administering medicine

- Helping individuals to use the toilet

- Just monitoring the individual, including periods of rest

Home and Motor Vehicle Modifications:

Home modifications that allow the accident victim to return home, despite his or her accident-related injuries are reimbursable.

- Constructing ramps

- Widening doors

- Lowering countertops

- Installing elevators

- Vehicle modifications such as wheelchair accessibility, that allow individuals to drive the motor vehicle, despite their accident, are also reimbursable.

Vocational Retraining:

The No-Fault law has historically been liberally construed to provide coverage for all types of reasonable expenses necessitated by a claimant's accident-related injury. For obvious reasons, determining what constitutes "reasonable and necessary expenses" has been the subject of much debate. The more serious the injury, the more incidental expenses will be covered, such as nursing home care and special arrangements to care properly for the claimant. Part of rehabilitative benefits can also include vocational and occupational rehabilitation. Insurance companies like to do everything possible to get an injured person back to some form of work to reduce their company's wage loss responsibility. Take note, however, this incentive **ends** near the three-year limitation for the insurance company to pay for work loss.

More than one Michigan case has held that reasonable expenses necessary for vocational rehabilitation are allowable expenses within the No-Fault Act. In cases where a claimant's injuries have left the claimant physically able to perform only sedentary work, the court has held that tuition and room and board costs may be reasonably necessary to provide the claimant with a vocation that allows for sedentary employment. In such a case, when the claimant's education is done, it allows the claimant to work and receive a salary that was at or even greater than the one he or she had earned before the accident.

NOTE: PIP benefits are usually payable when anyone is injured as a result of the ownership, operation, maintenance, or use of a motor vehicle. It needs to be kept in mind that a motor vehicle is defined as a vehicle with 4 wheels and therefore, does not cover an individual who is riding a motorcycle. That said, if an individual is riding a motorcycle and is struck by a motor vehicle, then No-Fault PIP benefits would be payable.

It's important to remember that health insurance does not cover many of these medical-related expenses. Michigan's No-Fault laws provided all types of different coverage under Section 3107(1)(a), to allow the injured individual to return as much as

possible to their lifestyle prior to the motor vehicle accident. Many court decisions interpreted the Michigan No-Fault law to provide coverage for such things as sending someone to school to learn a new trade so that they could afford to support themselves in the future. No such coverage, again, is available when someone simply has a healthcare policy or opts-out under the Medicare opt-out option.

CHAPTER FOURTEEN

NEW CHOICES TO MAKE

REGARDING "CAPS" ON REIMBURSEMENT LIMITS FOR MEDICAL-RELATED EXPENSES UNDER SECTION 3107(1)(a)

Now under Michigan's new No-Fault, individuals will be faced with deciding whether they wish to "save money" by purchasing different types of medical care coverage with caps on the amount of money that will be reimbursed to the individual to provide for medical-related expenses, or whether they will receive any coverage at all to be provided should they choose to opt-out of medical coverage.

Individuals will have choices, if they qualify, to select a medical expense cap of only $50,000 (the purchaser must be qualified to receive Medicaid), or caps of $250,000, $500,000, or a $250,000 excluder opt-out policy, or a Medicare opt-out option, or a managed care option. All of these options will be explained by insurance agents to Michigan consumers and cast as a potential "cost savings options." An example would be, "I can save you money and have your insurance premiums reduced if you elect not to have a lifetime medical care coverage." Or "you only pay for what you really need." The bottom line is that the only way Michigan consumers will be able to "save money" is <u>if they reduce the lifetime benefits they previously enjoyed by selecting some lesser type of option</u>.

It will take some time to interpret the language of the new laws adopted by the Michigan legislature and signed into law by Governor Whitmer. Some basic rules regarding the choices of coverage which all pertain to Personal Injury Protection (PIP benefits) are further described in the pages following in this book. The caps refer to $50,000, $250,000, and $500,000. These caps apply to each individual claiming benefits under the policy purchased. These caps are not an aggregate cap. If there is a different level of insurance coverage purchased in the same household, the higher level applies. There is no stacking of coverage from one individual to another. For any PIP benefit option or opt-out, the purchaser of insurance must be presented with a form based on language approved by Michigan's Department of Insurance and Financial Services (DIFS), which explains the benefits and risks of selecting any level of PIP coverage opt-out. This is required under Section 3107(c).

OPTIONS FOR REIMBURSMENT AVAILABLE FOR MEDICAL-RELATED EXPENSES UNDER SECTION 3107(1)(a)

THE $50,000 OPTION - INDIVIDUALS ELIGIBLE:

The $50,000 option caps reimbursement at $50,000 for medical-related expenses under Section 3107(1)(a) and is available only to those individuals who satisfy both of the following conditions:

- The person seeking such coverage is currently covered by Medicaid.

- The person's spouse and all resident relatives living in the same household are also on Medicaid, have other health insurance, or have PIP coverage through a different insurance policy. Again, this level of choice applies to the individual purchasing the insurance, the person's spouse, or any resident relative living in the home of the person purchasing such insurance coverage. *See Section 3107(c)(1)(a).*

OPTIONS FOR REIMBURSMENT AVAILABLE FOR MEDICAL-RELATED EXPENSES UNDER SECTION 3107(1)(a)

THE $250,000 OPTION - INDIVIDUALS ELIGIBLE:

*   This option caps reimbursement at $250,000 for medical-related expenses under Section 3107(1)(a), and is available to **any** person, without limitation. This level of choice applies to the person, the person's spouse, or any resident relative living in the purchaser's home. *See Section 3107(c)(1)(a).*

*   This option will likely be one of the most popular options for individuals who are not on Medicaid. It will likely be the least expensive option (other than managed care or individuals who are eligible for Medicare of Medicaid) that will be available to the purchaser of motor vehicle insurance coverage. It needs to be kept in mind, however, that an individual can easily go through $250,000 of medical expenses, sometimes even before ever getting out of the hospital when they have incurred serious motor vehicle accident injuries. If the individual's medical expenses exceed their cap, the person will then be on their own as to all of their own medical expenses unless they have another healthcare policy that might also provide coverage. Even if the individual does have another healthcare policy, many medical-related expenses that can be incurred by an

individual will not necessarily be covered by a healthcare insurance policy, even though their motor vehicle accident policy might have provided coverage for such expenses. When the $250,000 cap is reached, individuals will be on their own.

An individual can easily go through $250,000 of medical expenses, sometimes even before ever getting out of the hospital when they have incurred serious motor vehicle accident injuries.

OPTIONS FOR REIMBURSMENT AVAILABLE FOR MEDICAL-RELATED EXPENSES UNDER SECTION 3107(1)(a)

THE $250,000 EXCLUDER OPT-OUT OPTION
INDIVIDUALS ELIGIBLE:

- The Excluder Opt-out option caps reimbursement at $250,000 for all medical-related expenses, as provided by Section 3107(1)(a), and is available to individuals who, with his or her spouse, and all resident relatives living in the household, have other health insurance and accident insurance coverage that extends to auto-related injuries. Under this option, the insurer, under Section 3109(a)(2)(a), must offer an exclusion which reduces the insurance premium for the person's protection insurance benefits payable under Section 3107(1)(a) by 100%.

- If some resident relatives of the household do not have other coverage, then the exclusion can still be offered, but coverage must be factored in for those uncovered resident relatives.

- How this $250,000 exclusionary opt-out option will play out is uncertain at this time. Other language under Section 3109(a)(2)(C) is so broad as to provide concern that the exclusion sold under this section could bar payment of any and all PIP benefits, not just those reimbursable expenses under Section 3107(1)(a). The language of Section 3109(a)(2)(C) states "persons subject to an exclusion under this subsection are not eligible for personal protection benefits under the insurance policy." As an attorney, I must tell you that this language concerns me.

- **ACP (Assigned Claims Plan)** will not be available to individuals who select this option, should they be injured while an occupant of a motor vehicle (i.e., they are not necessarily the driver). However, those individuals selecting the $250,000 excluder opt-out could be entitled to coverage if they were injured while a non-occupant of a motor vehicle (i.e., a pedestrian or a bicyclist, or motorcyclist), where there is no other insurer, in terms of priority, which would provide PIP benefits to the injured individual.

- **There are certain rules for lapses in healthcare coverage that will come into play for those individuals selecting the $250,000 excluder opt-out.** If a $250,000 excluder opt-out has lapsed in their own health and accident insurance coverage, the individual is obligated to notify their no-fault insurer within 30 days of such lapse **and must purchase uncoordinated coverage. See Section 3109a(2)(d)**. If such a person is injured during this 30-day period, Section 3109a(2)(d)(ii) provides that the person will claim benefits through the **ACP**. That said, individuals claiming benefits through the **ACP** will have their benefits capped at $2 million. *Section 3172(7)(b)*. That said, it is not clear to me if this would be the scenario if the person had properly purchased the uncoordinated coverage prior to becoming injured within this 30-day timeframe. Likely, in such a case, the injured person would claim benefits under the newly purchased uncoordinated no-fault policy, but again, current no-fault laws do not spell this out.

- There are unanswered questions for all individuals selecting the $250,000 excluder opt-out option. The biggest one discussed thus far is what happens if the individual selecting the $250,000 excluder opt-out is injured and then subsequently loses healthcare coverage. This scenario could easily occur, especially during a period of unemployment as a result of serious injuries. Language in the new No-Fault law suggests that the excluder would not be entitled to any no-fault benefits and would either need to purchase other health insurance or be forced to rely on Medicaid or Medicare to provide medical-related benefits. As you can imagine, this is a very serious issue for individuals to be faced with. For this reason alone, I strongly advise against purchasing the $250,000 excluder opt-out option (until such time as our new No-Fault laws have been more thoroughly analyzed).

OPTIONS FOR REIMBURSMENT AVAILABLE FOR MEDICAL-RELATED EXPENSES UNDER SECTION 3107(1)(a)

THE $500,000 OPTION – INDIVIDUALS ELIGIBLE:

- Again, the $500,000 option caps reimbursement for all medical-related expenses under Section 3107(1)(a) and is an option available to **any** person without limitation. This level of choice applies to the individual purchasing insurance coverage, the person's spouse, or any resident relative living in the purchaser's household. *See Section 3107(c)(1)(c).*

- Again, many Michigan motorists will select this option of coverage because, while it will likely be a little more expensive than the $250,000 option, many motorists will see this as an in-between choice between the unlimited coverage and the $250,000 coverage, and will attempt to save some money when purchasing their insurance coverage.

- Again, the reader is reminded that in today's world, $500,000 in medical-related expenses can be reached in a relatively short time when an individual is catastrophically injured.

OPTIONS FOR REIMBURSMENT AVAILABLE FOR MEDICAL-RELATED EXPENSES UNDER SECTION 3107(1)(a)

THE LIFETIME OPTION (NO CAPS FOR REIMBURSEMENT FOR MEDICAL-RELATED EXPENSES):

- This option is again, available to **any** person without limitation and there is no cap on reimbursement for medical-related expenses under Section 3107(1)(a). This level of choice applies to the person, the person's spouse, or any resident relative living in the purchaser's household. *See Section 3107(c)(1)(d)*. One would think that purchasers of unlimited lifetime medical coverage should pay much <u>less</u> for their uninsured or underinsurance motorist benefits than people who buy capped PIP coverage policies, but nothing in the law requires this rate reduction to occur.

- I strongly recommend that people NOT be tempted to "save money" by selecting one of the lower caps options, either the $250,000 cap or the $500,000 cap (or even the $50,000 cap, or opting out entirely via the Medicare opt-out option). I realize that some people may not be able to afford purchasing this lifetime option of unlimited medical expenses coverage. That said, every time any of us gets behind the wheel or rides in a motor vehicle as a passenger, our lives are at the mercy of other drivers on the road. You can be the safest driver and still be injured, only because another driver has fallen asleep, suffered a heart attack, or engaged in reckless behavior such as texting or driving while under the influence of alcohol or drugs. Think of all the times that you have driven on a 2-lane highway and as you drove down the road at 50-60 mph, an oncoming vehicle whizzed by you driving at about the same speed only a few feet apart. Bad things can happen through no one's fault.

- Being seriously or catastrophically injured in a motor vehicle accident is always life-threatening. Whether it's pain and suffering or restrictions on mobility, a serious injury from a motor vehicle accident has lifetime consequences. When calculating "taking a chance" on not being seriously injured as a result of a motor vehicle accident, keep in mind that insurance statistics indicate that during their lifetime, 1 out of every 38 motor vehicle drivers will end up being in a serious motor vehicle accident where an individual is seriously injured.

Based on my knowledge gained from helping people for over 30 years involved in motor vehicle accidents, I strongly suggest that if possible, individuals purchase the lifetime option when selecting their motor vehicle PIP coverage.

OPTIONS FOR REIMBURSMENT AVAILABLE FOR MEDICAL-RELATED EXPENSES UNDER SECTION 3107(1)(a)

THE MANAGED CARE OPTION

- Managed care option means an optional coverage selected by an insured at the time a policy is issued which includes, but is not limited to, the monitoring and adjudication of an injured person's care, the use of a provider program, or other network, or other similar option. Section 3181.

- Insurers in Michigan could begin selling the managed care option beginning on June 11, 2019. All No-Fault insurers are allowed to offer managed care option plans, Section 3182.

- The managed care option applies to the insured who selected the managed care option and to any person who resided in an area where the managed care option is available and was claiming PIP benefits under the managed care policy. Section 3185.

- PIP benefits under a managed care plan must be exhausted before a person can seek medical benefits from another health or accident coverage provider, Section 3187(b).

- The language of Section 3183 attempts to mirror the language found in Section 3107a by stating that, "an automobile insurer may offer a managed care option that provides for allowable expenses consisting of all reasonable charges incurred for reasonably necessary products, services, and accommodations for an injured person's care, recovery, or rehabilitation."

- The key part of managed care is that the care must be provided through the use "of a preferred provider program or other network or other similar option." In essence, this means that "your care, your doctor, your rehabilitation center, your chiropractor, and your physical therapist, etc.," would be *selected by your insurance company*. Since you could only select from individuals that were deemed to be "a preferred provider," or in a program or another network that the insurance company had previously approved of, i.e., the insurance company would set its fees and indicate what type of services and how many visits could be allowed, etc.

- I want to emphasize that the managed option is a terrible idea that should be avoided at all costs by the consumer.

THE WORK LOSS OPT-OUT OPTION FOR RETIREES OR OLDER NON-EMPLOYED INDIVIDUALS

THE WORK LOSS OPT-OUT OPTION

- Under Section 3107(2)(a), "a person who is 60 years of age or older and in the event of an accidental bodily injury, would not be eligible to receive work loss benefits under

Section 3107(1)(b)" (i.e., an individual not working and not able to establish a future wage loss) "may waive coverage for work loss benefits by signing a waiver on a form provided by the insurer. An insurer shall offer a reduced premium rate to a person who waives coverage under this Subsection for work loss benefits. Waiver of coverage for work loss benefits applies only to work loss benefits payable to the person or persons who have signed the waiver form."

• Often individuals 60 years of age may contemplate retiring in the near future and be led to think this is another way to "save money." That said, the truth is that as people age into their 60's, many individuals change their mind and decide they cannot afford to retire...and then they are injured. So, my advice is not to waive this important coverage until *after* you have been retired for some time and then only when you have determined that you will not be returning to any part-time or full-time employment.

OPTIONS FOR EXTRA COVERAGE FOR AT HOME ATTENDANT CARE

ATTENDANT CARE RIDERS?

• Insurers providing policies with limits of $50,000, $250,000 or $500,000 shall offer "a rider that

will provide coverage for attendant care in excess of the applicable limit."

• This rider does not <u>require</u> the sale of attendant care coverage in excess of the 56 weekly hourly limitations set forth in the new law at Section 3157(10), and further referred to in Section 3107c(8). **Current language in the new No-Fault law does not appear to set an amount of attendant care that has to be covered under such a rider.**

• Section 3107c(9) states "an insurer **shall** offer, **for a policy that provides the security required under section 3101(1) to which a limit under subsection (1)(a)(2)(c) applies, [$50,000, $250,000, $500,000 caps]** a rider that will provide coverage for attendant care in excess of the applicable limit." Nothing is mentioned about requiring such a rider for someone that selects coverage under Section 3107c(1)(d) [no limit for personal protection insurance benefits under Section 3107(1)(a)]. This makes no sense! An unanswered question is that when somebody elects to have the best medical care coverage, are they still limited by Section 3157(10) to 8 hours a day 7 days a week of attendant care? Does that mean that an insurance carrier that sells one of their policy holders the best medical coverage available does not have to provide a rider for providing for additional attendant care coverage?

• The important thing to know under Section 3157(10) is that attendant care coverage (taking care of a person in the person's own home) cannot be performed in excess of 8 hours per day, if such care is provided by any of the following:

a. An individual who is related to the injured person;

b. An individual who is domiciled in the household of the injured person; or

c. An individual with whom the injured person <u>had</u> a business or social relationship <u>before</u> their injury.

- Again, under section 3157(11), an insured may contract to pay for more hours under subsection 11 (if the insurer thinks it's in their best financial interest to do so). In other words, if the insurance company's representative thinks they can save money by hiring one of those identified individuals in section 3157(10), they have the option of doing so, but they are not required to do so. Make sure to discuss this issue with the agent that you are purchasing your insurance policy from, if you want the option to have attendant care provided for you, for more than 8 hours a day by one of those individuals excluded under section 3157(10).

BASIC RULES REGARDING PIP CHOICE OPT-OUTS

- <u>**Monetary caps on allowable expense enefit**</u>: Monetary caps apply to Section 3107(1)(a) medical-related allowable expense benefits only. These caps do not apply to wage loss, replacement services, or survivor loss benefits.

- **Caps apply to individuals:** The insurance coverage cap selected applies to each individual claiming benefits under the policy that provides coverage. It is not an aggregate cap.

- **Largest cap applies:** If different levels of cap coverage exist in a household, the higher level selected by a household member applies. That said, there is no stacking of one insurance policy with another.

- **Basic rules regarding PIP choice opt-outs:** Pursuant to Section 3107c(2), for any PIP benefit option or opt-out, the person purchasing insurance must be presented with a form document promulgated by the Department of Insurance and Financial Services (DIFS) that explain the "benefits and risks" of selecting any level of PIP coverage or opt-out.

CHAPTER FIFTEEN

UMBRELLA POLICIES

What is an umbrella insurance policy? This is a type of policy which provides personal liability coverage for claims that exceed the limits of the policy owner's regular auto, watercraft, or homeowners' insurance policies. Such umbrella coverage protects your personal assets from being reached from a lawsuit, should you or a permissive driver of your insured vehicle cause a catastrophic injury or death of another person.

Whether it makes sense to purchase an umbrella policy depends on whether you have significant assets to protect. When you have assets to protect of at least $1 million (real estate, cash, investments, etc.) it certainly makes sense to have an umbrella policy. Depending on the language of the umbrella policy, claims for other causes of action may also be covered (i.e., liable, slander, false arrest, liabilities on rental properties you may own, etc.).

Accordingly, if it's a close question, I always recommend that Michigan consumers consider purchasing large umbrella policies to protect themselves from being sued for excess medical expenses that exceed an injured party's cap that may have been selected by someone seriously injured in a motor vehicle. For example, if you seriously injure someone and they have selected a cap of only $50,000 or $250,000, and their medical expenses exceed the cap they selected, you will likely be opening yourself up for being sued by that injured party for their excess medical expenses, as well as any excess wage loss. A number of Michigan citizens who are on Medicare may have chosen to opt-out of any auto insurance coverage for their medical-related expenses and they may have many medical-related expenses that are not covered by their healthcare insurance or Medicare, as the case may be.

Under Michigan's *old* No-Fault laws, all Michigan residents were required to purchase unlimited medical expense coverage, and drivers who caused accidents where people were seriously injured were protected from ever being sued for excess medical-related expenses by a party they injured. **That is not the case anymore.** Accordingly, when people have opted out of coverage or selected the options of lower insurance caps, if such an individual is seriously or catastrophically injured in a motor vehicle accident, you can expect that they may end up suing the at-fault driver for their excess medical expense that are not covered under the insurance coverage policy they opted to purchase.

Accordingly, I also strongly suggest that individuals who consider themselves financially secure consider purchasing a $1 million, $2 million, or even a $5 million umbrella insurance policy. If such an umbrella policy is available to you, having the same in place will protect you should you, or someone you allowed to drive your insured motor vehicle, seriously injure someone else in a motor vehicle accident. Umbrella policies can also provide coverage for accidents occurring outside of Michigan, as well as in foreign countries when your auto policy might not provide coverage. In order to purchase a large umbrella policy, the consumer may also be required to purchase a high bodily injury liability coverage. Minimum bodily injury insurance policies typically require coverage of at least the recommended $250,000 minimum, or a minimum coverage of $500,000 or even $1 million, as the case may be (depending on the limits of the umbrella policy that you are seeking to purchase).

CHAPTER SIXTEEN

SUMMARY OF MY RECOMMENDATIONS TO BE ADEQUATELY INSURED

INSURANCE COVERAGE	**Reimbursement for Medical-Related expenses Under Section 3107(1)(a)**
RECOMMENDED MINIMUM AMOUNT	Unlimited is the best of course, but a cap of no less than $500,000 is my recommendation
FOR	Reimbursement for Medical-Related expenses, including home modifications, vocational training, ambulance charges, etc., up to the cap you select.
NOTES	If you are catastrophically injured, having an unlimited cap will prevent you from being forced into bankruptcy or on Medicaid or both. Consider purchasing an attendant care rider, if available, at a low cost.

INSURANCE COVERAGE	**Bodily Injury (BI)**
RECOMMENDED MINIMUM AMOUNT	Suggested minimum of $250,000/$500,000 coverage. That said, my recommendation is to purchase a higher amount of coverage (at least a $500,000 single limit coverage) if you are trying to protect sizeable assets, wish to purchase a high amount of UM coverage, or wish to purchase an umbrella policy where UM coverage is included.
FOR	Coverage for other person's injuries when you cause an accident.
NOTES	Provides protection for your personal assets. It also provides eligibility for you to purchase uninsured/underinsured motorist coverage. It does not cover expenses for your bodily injuries. The amount of minimum coverage per individual you purchase (i.e., $50,000, $100,000, $250,000 or $500,000) will also often dictate the amount of UM coverage you are eligible to purchase to protect yourself and your family members. Your insurance agent can explain his/her company's requirements regarding UM coverage limits.
IINSURANCE COVERAGE	**Property Damage Insurance (PPI)**
RECOMMENDED MINIMUM AMOUNT	$1 million coverage for accidents occurring in Michigan and $10,000 for accidents occurring outside of Michigan. The $1 million is the minimum required for accidents occurring in Michigan, and I would not increase this coverage. That said, see my comments below if you frequently drive out of state.
FOR	Damage you caused to another's property (other than their motor vehicle, unless it was legally parked).

NOTES

It does not cover damages to your vehicle or to another motor vehicle unless the other motor vehicle was legally parked. If you frequently drive out of state, discuss with your insurance agent increasing property damage coverage limits for an out of state accident.

INSURANCE
COVERAGE

UM coverage

RECOMMENDED
MINIMUM AMOUNT

I suggest purchasing, if possible, at least $500,000 of UM coverage. This amount of coverage will usually make you eligible to purchase a larger umbrella policy. Check with your insurance agent regarding his/her requirements for purchasing umbrella policies.

FOR

Protection for you and your family, if injured in an accident caused by a driver with no insurance or limited bodily injury insurance.

NOTES

Having underinsured motorist coverage can be the most important coverage you purchase to protect you and your family members.

NSURANCE
COVERAGE

Mini tort coverage

RECOMMENDED
MINIMUM AMOUNT

If you purchase this coverage it will provide coverage for up to $3,000 for damage caused to another party's motor vehicle.

FOR

Protects you, financially, if you are at-fault in causing damage to another person's motor vehicle while you or a permissive driver is operating your motor vehicle.

NOTES

This type of coverage is very inexpensive and should be purchased by you.

INSURANCE
COVERAGE

Collision Insurance

RECOMMENDED
MINIMUM AMOUNT

The cost depends on the age and value of your vehicle to be insured. Unless your vehicle has very little value this coverage should be purchased. If you owe money on your insured vehicle, the lending institution typically <u>requires</u> that you purchase this coverage and name them as an additional insured.

FOR

Covers damage to your vehicle caused by a collision while being operated.

NOTES

It does not matter who was at-fault for causing the accident and damage to your vehicle. With broad collision coverage, if the other party is at-fault, you don't pay for any deductible.

INSURANCE
COVERAGE

Comprehensive Insurance

RECOMMENDED
MINIMUM AMOUNT

The cost depends on the age and value of your vehicle.

FOR

Covers damages to your vehicle when it is being stored (fire/theft coverage). Covers damage to your vehicle not covered by a collision insurance.

NOTES

Does not cover any vehicle damage resulting from a collision with another vehicle when being operated by you or a permissive driver.

CONCLUSION

In this book I have done my best to provide information to you, the consumer, regarding decisions that will need to be intelligently made when purchasing a motor vehicle insurance policy in light of Michigan's new No-Fault laws. Throughout this book I have referred to auto insurance interchangeably with motor vehicle insurance. There are a lot of truck drivers out there!

Additionally, as I am finalizing this book, the citizens of our great country have been heroically responding to the crisis caused by the Coronavirus (COVID-19) pandemic. Whether Michigan's legislature deems it to be in the best interest of our citizens to delay the effective date of Michigan's new No-Fault laws from July 1, 2020 to some later date, perhaps 90-120 days down the road, remains to be seen. Doing so might be wise to give Michigan consumers some additional time to meet with their insurance agents, face-to-face, to understand the complexities of the new options available for them to select when purchasing their auto insurance policies for the next year. Making hasty decisions on the opt-outs could come back to haunt individuals. Taking a little additional time might have prevented regrets from occurring.

It is my understanding that in 2020 when insurance policies are being renewed, and such renewal extends over July 1, 2020, insurance companies will automatically be including unlimited PIP coverage when it comes to reimbursement for medical-related expenses. Such renewals will also automatically include bodily injury coverage limits of at least $250,000/$500,000. Michigan's Department of Financial Information (DIFS) is promulgating forms for consumers to sign declining such coverages (unlimited reimbursement for medical-related expenses and/or the recommended $250,000/$500,000 bodily injury coverage). These forms are expected to be distributed mid-May 2020. That being said, in light of COVID-19, I am not sure whether consumers will have enough time to fully appreciate the ramifications of selecting different options that will be available to them "to save money" under Michigan's new no-fault laws.

Regardless of whether the effective date remains July 1, 2020 or is extended to a later date, hopefully by having read this book, Michigan consumers will have gained the knowledge necessary to help them better decide what is best for them and their family members when it comes time to buying auto insurance. In looking out for the individual consumer, I have made certain recommendations such as protecting assets by purchasing large umbrella policies. Moreover, for those that want peace of mind and can afford it, I recommend purchasing the unlimited option when it comes to reimbursement for medical-related expenses.

It also needs to be kept in mind that when individuals purchase reimbursement for medical-related expense PIP coverage, under Section 3107(1)(a), such protection covers many medical-related expenses beyond basic healthcare expenses (i.e., vocational training, home modifications for individuals with ambulatory problems, etc.). These additional medical-related services help the seriously injured individual live <u>as nearly as possible the lives that they enjoyed before being injured</u>. This type of reimbursement for medical-related expenses protection cannot be purchased by any other form of insurance. This is an especially important consideration for older individuals on Medicare who will be considering the option of whether to completely opt-out of the reimbursement for medical-related expenses in their PIP coverage.

So, while it is a cost savings, and it while it may be deemed a necessary choice for those living on a <u>very</u> limited budget, I still recommend against such a Medicare opt-out. Each individual has to make choices in life, and this is one that I go on record in discouraging. No one can predict the likelihood of being injured. No one could have predicted COVID-19 changing the way we live in America, just as no one can predict whether you might be seriously injured in a motor vehicle accident. By keeping No-Fault coverage for reimbursement of medical-related expenses under Section 3107(1)(a), at least you can have the peace of mind that comes from having a level of protection that is not otherwise available from Medicare or healthcare coverage.

So, while I realize that economics will always play a role in the decision-making process when selecting options under Michigan's new No-Fault laws, I caution against focusing too much on potential cost savings and resist responding to the slogan "purchase only what you need." No one can rationally justify such a statement, because you only know what you need **after you have been involved in an accident which has caused you to be seriously injured - - and then it's too late**.

My best and God Bless!

How to Subscribe to Barberi Law's Newsletter or Get it Sent to a Friend or Family Member

If you are reading this book, you might also be receiving our monthly hardcopy newsletter which covers interesting stories about the law, news items that we believe you will find very useful and interesting, and other information to keep you up-to-date on relevant changes to Michigan's new No-Fault laws.

If you would like to recommend family and/or friends who you believe might also be interested in receiving our newsletter, simply provide us with their names and addresses. We would be delighted to reach more interested individuals. We'll send each of them our monthly newsletter, along with a note telling them that you graciously referred them. Don't worry, we don't share information with any other parties! (If, for any reason, they don't want to receive it, there is always a toll-free number that can be called to remove a name from the subscription list.)

If you are not receiving our newsletter and would like to, we'll be happy to sign you up for a free subscription.

Subscribing Is Easy

Call with names and addresses (and email addresses if available), or send requests via fax, email, or standard mail.

Call:

989-773-3423

Email:

admin@barberilawfirm.com

Fax:

989-772-6444

Mail:

Barberi Law

2305 Hawthorn Drive, Ste. C, Mt. Pleasant, MI 48858

*We also have an email version of the newsletter, and if you prefer receiving your copy in your inbox, simply provide us with your email address.

We Appreciate Your Referrals

Thank You for Your Trust and Confidence

IMPORTANT DISCLAIMER

On July 1, 2020, most of the new No-Fault Laws will become effective. To help consumers make informed decisions when selecting PIP options, I've rushed publication of this book. Proofreading was kept at a minimum and mistakes can occur when acting quickly. My hope is that such unintended error will be insignificant in nature and that those observant readers finding error will be both understanding and forgiving. Some of the language of the new laws is unclear and in need of clarification. Over the next few months, I expect amendments to be made and my interpretation of what the laws state will also likely change. Accordingly, readers are encouraged to drop me a line with any suggestions for my next edition!

ABOUT THE AUTHOR

Joseph Barberi has been practicing auto accident injury law in the Central Michigan area for over thirty years. Prior to entering private practice, Mr. Barberi served as the elected Prosecuting Attorney for Isabella County for 12 years. During his tenure, he was also elected by his peers to serve as President of the Prosecuting Attorney's Association of Michigan. By virtue of this position, Mr. Barberi worked with Michigan's Attorney General and Governor concerning criminal justice issues, some of which involved enforcement of Michigan's Motor Vehicle Code.

Mr. Barberi has tried hundreds of jury trials and won all but three. He holds Isabella County's record for the largest single jury verdict in a motor vehicle accident case. In addition, he has settled over a thousand motor vehicle accident cases, many for millions and multiple millions of dollars each. Mr. Barberi employs jury consultants both before and during litigation, and has, on several occasions, conducted mock jury trials during litigation to ascertain the likely maximum jury value of a particular case.

Mr. Barberi is a member of Michigan's Association of Justice and has lectured at Michigan Association of Justice seminars. He has addressed members of the Michigan Association of Justice regarding the use of digital motion x-ray (DMX) to document ligamentous and tendon injuries sustained by individuals during motor vehicle accidents. Mr. Barberi has also conducted trial tactic seminars on jury selection and opening statements.

Mr. Barberi is also a well-known trial attorney in other areas of personal injury law. In addition to handling motor vehicle accident cases (including truck accidents and motorcycle accidents), Mr. Barberi also handles medical malpractice claims, serious dog bite cases, and premises liability claims.

BARBERI LAW

EVERY CASE WE TAKE,
WE TAKE PERSONALLY.®

2305 HAWTHORN DRIVE, STE C,
MT. PLEASANT, MI 48858

989-773-3423
1-800-336-3423

WWW.BARBERILAWFIRM.COM

WA